12 Businesses That People Can Start Online In 1 Day Or Less!

Are you ready to start making money online?

The time is now!

By: Tolga CAKIR

First Printing: 2020

ISBN 978-0-9933038-4-5

Black Eagle Publishing Ltd.

71 -75 Shelton Street Covent Garden

LONDON, UK

WC2H 9JQ

www.blackeaglepublishing.co.uk

Claim Your Free Bonus

www.tolgacakir.com/bonus

Table of Contents

1. A Message from the Author

This book features some of the best online business ideas that can be implemented right away! We want to bring you all these great ideas and all these awesome tips in one convenient book, as well as open you up to different ideas that you can easily implement in a short amount of time – whether it be to start a new business or add a new income stream to an existing one of yours.

PART 1:

THE ONES YOU'VE PROBABLY THOUGHT OF

"There's more than one way to make money online?"

Okay, maybe this isn't quite the question you find yourself asking, but if you are like most people, the idea that there are twelve ways (*twelve ways!*) to make money online—to make money online *quickly*, no less—may seem like a foreign concept. After all, it seems that so many people are always trying and failing to make money online, right? If there are so many ways to approach this holy grail of wealth creation, then, why are so many people left wondering what they are missing in their quest to reach this end result in their own life?

The truth, however, is that there are plenty of ways in which you can take your computer, hop online, and start making money, and within each "way you can take your computer, hop online, and start making money," there are countless subcategories you can explore to find exactly the right approach for you. The issue most people run into in their failed quests to make money online is not that they are unable to figure out an approach to take ... but is instead that they fail to realize that there is more to making money online than simply settling on an approach that works best for you.

As with any form of wealth creation, making money online will require effort. Sometimes, it will require quite a bit of effort! But, as the saying goes, "it sure beats working!"

In order to succeed online, you are going to have to be willing to learn the ins and outs of the approach you have chosen to take. You have to be willing to try and fail. And you have to be willing to pick yourself up if you do fail — to dust yourself off, and to start over again. Why is this important to realize? Because, quite simply, once you grasp the concepts behind making money online, and once you figure out the approach that works for you, it all becomes quite easy!

In this short, powerful book, we will lay out for you twelve different ways you can go about making money online. Some of these businesses will require more work than others. Some of these businesses will have a faster payoff than others, while others will have a higher ceiling. All of these online business ideas have one thing in common, however: they are each easy to set up, easy to get started with, and easy to make money with if you are willing to put in the work to get things going!

Does that mean that you won't run into any hurdles? Almost certainly not! Will this book contain absolutely everything you'll need to perfect each of these ideas? Certainly not! As no business idea or concept is ever perfect – they're always evolving, requiring tweaks and testing, etc.. But this book is meant to open your eyes to the possibilities of what's out there so you can take any of the concepts here, try them out relatively easily, and get a feel for them hopefully within a day or less! This doesn't mean they'll all be perfect within a day or that you'll be making major bank within a day in every single case, but it does mean that you can get them started and grow from there all without a ton of time or upfront investment on your part!

In this first section — the first several businesses we are going to look at — we will be exploring some of the more common approaches to creating wealth online. These approaches are the ones that tend to come to mind first for those who focus on Internet marketing for a full-time living. While these first several online business ideas may be the ones that would come to mind first for most successful online entrepreneurs, however, that does not necessarily mean that these will be the best businesses for you.

In order to join the group of individuals who have made the Internet their place of business — and who have made their home their office, and have made "whatever they feel like wearing" their uniform — you need to find the approach you feel most comfortable taking. Perhaps you will find that approach among the twelve explored in this book, or perhaps the ideas in this book will inspire you to explore another, related area of online wealth creation (there are TONS). Regardless of the approach you decide is best for yourself, however, realize this:

Everyone has the ability to make money online — and that includes you!

Once you settle on an approach you feel will be a perfect fit for you, you will be able to jump on board, will be able to have your business set up in less than a day, and will be able to start putting in the time and effort required to get this business off the ground, and to start making massive amounts of income (often of the "passive income" variety!) from the comfort of your bathrobe and your favorite recliner, in your home, on your own schedule — living the life most people only ever dream of living!

2.   1. E-Commerce Store

What this online business looks like

Sure, you know about websites where you can go to do your shopping. You've probably made your fair share of purchases from Amazon, or even from sites such as Best Buy. But did you realize that you have probably also made purchases from sites being run by someone who never touches or deals with any of the products themselves?

With an e-commerce store, you can basically pick a category of products (the category can be broad or small, and can include lots of items or a select few in a very specific niche), and you can set up a website on which people can do their shopping. Although you will, obviously, not receive a large chunk of the profits from each sale made through your website (after all, your website is essentially functioning as nothing more than a platform on which people can make purchases of someone else's products), you will also have to do very little work to make the money you will be making (specifically, you will have to do none of the "labor" yourself—none of the manufacturing of products, none of the packaging of products, none of the shipping of products, etc.). All you will have to do is set up your e-commerce website, figure out ways to bring targeted traffic your way, and then enjoy the profits as they roll in!

What you need to get started

There are plenty of e-commerce platforms to choose from, and all of them make it easy for you to set up your site and get started right away (in fact, with the various options available for starting an e-commerce site, one of the main ways in which these sites aim to compete with one another is by making their particular platform the easiest to work with—which is great news for you, as this means you will not only have options, but that all your options will also be for platforms that are easy to get started with!). We are going to give you a list of five of the preeminent e-commerce platforms, and we encourage you to check out each one for yourself, and to decide which one offers the product with which you feel most comfortable!

Here are the five e-commerce platforms we have found to be the strongest (listed in no particular order):

- Shopify

- Magento

- Bigcommerce

- WooCommerce

- 3dcart

Another big one worth mentioning is Amazon.com itself, as you can list products through there either to ship independently or have them be directly fulfilled by Amazon as well. There are major pros and cons to having it on Amazon vs. another site. First, having it on Amazon is a great way for people to organically find your products. However, you also don't have a lot of control over it, pay big fees to Amazon, can't easily have upsells or backend offers, can't as easily build a list from it, etc.. All of this somewhat limits the products that might be most ideal for this.

Where to find your products

There are lots of ways to find products for you to sell on your e-commerce site! And the cool part is that you don't even have to pay for them upfront (unless you want to). You can do what's called dropshipping, which is basically where your customer pays you your retail price, and then you pay a wholesaler to dropship it for you. One very big site for this is Aliexpress.com!

The cool part with Aliexpress is that you can search for any type of product you want, and then you can even sort by the popularity of the products to give you new ideas about what might sell well (as well as related products to also offer). Depending upon the product type and the niche, you can also have some extremely high margins, which is often rare in the e-commerce business. For instance, you can find jewelry that costs $1 or less (including free shipping) that many would consider a steal at $10 or $20. Or products that might normally go for $1,000 or more, you can often find for significantly less (making it easier for you to profit off of it).

The downside with dropshipping from overseas like with Aliexpress is that it can sometimes take several weeks to a month or more to be received elsewhere in the world, but it's a good alternative to having to buy lots of inventory ahead of time and storing it all. I would only suggest buying lots of inventory if you already have some winners that are selling well and you want to really grow the business. Then you can use Aliexpress' sister site, Alibaba.com, and find wholesalers that will ship you the product in bulk to sell from your house or warehouse, but I would only recommend that once you already have an established product or two making a lot of sales.

Extra Tips and Tricks

One thing that you can do to take this concept to the next level is to look for super cheap items that you can sell for a "free plus shipping & handling" model where you actually can make a little profit when you have your prospects just pay the s&h! For instance, you can find jewelry that you can get from Aliexpress for $1 or $2 that includes worldwide s&h, which you can turn around and sell for "free plus $4.95 s&h" to pocket a few dollars on. But you don't want to stop there!

You can step it up a notch by using this as a way to get prospects to open their wallets to you (because it's an unbeatable deal in their eyes), but then have a series of upsell offers where they can buy related products but at higher prices with higher margins. Using the jewelry as an example, perhaps the earrings are free plus s&h, but you try to upsell them into a matching necklace, bracelet, and/or ring with prices ranging from more free plus $4.95 or higher upfront prices like $10 to $30. This greatly increases the average purchase price where you can go from making a few bucks to making $20+ per buyer. You can also have recurring memberships into a monthly "jewelry club" (or whatever product type you're selling) or even much higher priced offers when relevant. These "free plus s&h" offers can also be killer to do paid ads on, as they're great deals that get people to open their wallets.

What your expectations should be

Is making money with an e-commerce site as simple as just setting up the site and watching as the profits roll in? Of course not! If it were this easy, after all, everyone could set up an e-commerce site in less than a day and be rolling in dough in no time at all! While getting set up with an e-commerce site is as easy as anything, the key to success in e-commerce is bringing traffic your way!

The good news? This is not as difficult as you might have thought!

While one approach to bringing traffic to your e-commerce site is to do some search engine optimization on your site to bring organic traffic your way, another — quicker, easier — approach is to simply spend up on some ads like through Adwords and Facebook! By targeting specific buyer keywords in a set of Adwords ads, you can target traffic that will be likely to purchase the products on your site. And with Facebook ads, you can target people who might be more likely to have an interest in your products with a very targeted offer. Sure, this will require a bit of an investment upfront, but this investment can turn into a profit quickly, and can jumpstart your quest to become a successful online business owner! Investing a bit in ads can also be a great way to find out sooner if you have a winner or not so you can make adjustments from there instead of waiting and seeing if you'll get lucky.

3. 2. Affiliate Marketing: Goods

What this online business looks like

Affiliate marketing — have you heard of it? If you have been around the Internet marketing game for any significant time at all, you are probably sick of hearing about affiliate marketing, frankly, as it seems to be all anyone talks about! But in case you are new to internet marketing, we will give you a brief background (and even if you are not new to Internet marketing — and you think you already know all there is to know about the basics of affiliate marketing — we encourage you to read this section in its entirety, as we have a few important tidbits to share that will help you on your way to success!).

Basically, with affiliate marketing, your efforts will be centered around promoting the products of others. This is similar to e-commerce, except that affiliate marketing is not based around the idea of people making purchases on your website. Instead, the purpose of your site will be to send people to another site where they will make a purchase—and each time someone makes a purchase as a result of your efforts, you will receive what amounts to a "commission" for the sale.

What you need to get started

Who can you be an affiliate for? If this is something you are wondering, you might be surprised by the answer … as the answer is, frankly, you can be an affiliate for just about any company or product you can think of! Just about every business that has an online presence also has an affiliate marketing program — and all of them work different ways.

For example, Amazon's affiliate marketing program: As an Amazon affiliate, you can promote any product they sell on their site (which pretty much gives you a choice of every type of product you can think of). Amazon tracks traffic that you send to their site, and any purchase someone makes during their visit to Amazon (the visit you sent them on) will be credited to you. While this may seem like a great route to go, however, one of the drawbacks to Amazon's affiliate program is that Amazon is tremendously popular without the help of affiliates! Because of this, Amazon does not need to offer large "commissions" — and what's more, a purchase has to be made directly from the visit to Amazon that you created. Any purchases made on Amazon a day later, or even a few hours later, will not be credited to you.

Other websites, on the other hand, will store cookies and track traffic for as long as six months. So, for example, say you sent someone to a website for private jet booking, and that individual booked a private jet four months later. Because you sent that individual to the site four months earlier, you would receive your affiliate commission!

In order to get started, then, you simply need to figure out the niche in which you want to focus, and need to then find a great affiliate program with which to team up. It's really that simple! Pick a niche — any niche — and you should be able to find an affiliate marketing program to match.

Tricks to making affiliate marketing easier

Most people who fail at affiliate marketing, especially when they don't have an e-mail list, a website, or anything to start with, typically do so because they just throw up an affiliate link and hope that people will buy. This rarely ever works.

You typically have to offer value first and foremost to your prospects! That means if someone is looking to buy a moped, they likely have a lot of questions not only on mopeds in general, but also on what models to buy, where to buy them from online, etc., which you could help answer along with suggestions (aka your affiliate links) on where they should buy and why. For instance, you could write up a blog post or an article on what to look for in a moped, what they might want if it's just them or if they'd have a passenger, if it's just around town for super short distances or much further, etc., and then offer suggestions (via your affiliate link) on models that would best work for them! This kind of helpful affiliate marketing can work incredibly well, as your helping prospects make a buying decision and leading them to an offer that you get paid on (just make sure your suggestion legitimately is good).

So you might be wondering how you find such prospects or get traffic to your helpful posts or videos like this? Well, there's a couple main ways… First, you can try to rank on Google and the like for search terms that prospects might be searching for. For instance, using the moped example, you could target keywords like "what is a good moped for two people," "150cc vs. 250 cc engines in mopeds," "best cheap mopeds," "where to buy mopeds online," or "what to look for in a moped." You can put these keywords as the title of your blog post, the title of your video, etc. and have a good chance of ranking, especially with the resources mentioned in the intro of this book.

The second way is to don't wait for prospects to find you, but for you to go out and find your prospects. So instead of waiting to get ranked, you could go to popular forums, blogs, Q&A sites (like Quora.com, Yahoo Answers, etc.), social media, etc. where prospects are already hanging out and asking relevant questions, and then simply take a minute to answer them! You can drive the traffic back to your site or video with your useful info, recommendation, and affiliate link. All of these kinds of sites make it super easy to search them for relevant questions that you can then take the time to answer in a helpful manner, yet very few people take the time to do so, which is not only being lazy, but likely losing them a lot of money! That's because a single answer doesn't just potentially get you one prospect – it can get you dozens, hundreds, or even thousands or more seeing the answer you publicly gave and checking our your site, video, or link later. The key is to give value first, drive them to your post or video, and then have the link on that post / site or video along with super helpful info! If you can do that, you're way ahead of likely 99% of the competition.

What your expectations should be

As with an e-commerce site, you will still need to create traffic to your site in order to be successful. And as with an e-commerce site, you can use search engine optimization or Adwords (or Facebook) to create this traffic. As soon as you start receiving traffic, you can start turning a profit!

The biggest key most people miss when it comes to affiliate marketing, however (and the reason we advised you to stick around even if you think you understand affiliate marketing), is that it's always better to target high-end products in your affiliate marketing efforts!

Generally speaking, it is just as easy to make a single sale of a high-priced item as it is to make a single sale of a low-priced item. Because the affiliate commission will be so much higher on a high-priced item, then, the biggest key to success is to always target those high-end products that will bring you those high-end commissions!

4.   3. Affiliate Marketing: Information Products

What this online business looks like

Information products are one of the easiest ways to make money online, as people are always looking to learn more about topics in which they are interested (and honestly, one of the most popular areas of information products deals with products that help people learn how to make money online!).

Information products, essentially, are exactly what they sound like: they are non-physical goods that provide people with knowledge rather than an actual item. "How to become an online millionaire" is a general idea of what an information product might look like. "How to triple traffic to your website in three weeks" might be a more specific information product.

Of course, one great way to generate money online is to create information products yourself. But even if you do not have the expertise to create your own information products, you can become an affiliate for information products, and can make a large sum of money simply promoting the information products others have put together!

What you need to get started

First, you need to determine the area in which you want to focus. Then, you need an audience! An audience, of course, can come together through a website, but another way to build an audience can be through a newsletter. If you are able to build a newsletter with a subscriber list populated with individuals who have an interest in a specific area, it will be very easy to sell information products in this area to those on your mailing list!

That's why it's always important to be building an e-mail list so that you can sell to them later – whether it be affiliate products or offers of your own! A list is a huge asset that you can profit off of for years to come, and they're very cheap and easy to get started. Autoresponder services like Aweber, GetResponse, etc. typically cost in the $10 to $15 / month range (there are some free and even cheaper options out there, but they aren't always highly recommended), yet they can be used to generate massive profits. And you can start building them simply by giving people a good reason to join your list (whether it be for discounts, a free report, free software, some other free offer, a newsletter, free tips / advice, etc.).

Below, you will find a list of some of the most popular "digital product" platforms. Once you determine the area in which you want to focus, you can figure out which network of digital products is the best fit for you:

Clickbank

Mooshpay

JVZoo

WarriorPlus

What your expectations should be

The expectation for success in affiliate marketing of information products is going to be similar to the expectation for success in e-commerce and in affiliate marketing of tangible goods: you need to generate traffic (or have a targeted audience) in order to turn a profit in this area … but once you are able to build a targeted audience, you will be able to start making a lot of money with very little effort! In fact, selling information products can often create the quickest turnaround time between "getting started" and "seeing big profits" in your online business efforts!

The same marketing tips and tricks mentioned in the prior affiliate marketing section will also apply here (getting ranked, going straight to prospects, etc.), so rather than repeat that, just make sure to read the prior business idea just in case under the marketing tricks section. However, one additional trick that can work well for digital products in affiliate marketing is to offer a bonus if they buy through your link. This can be an additional free report, tool, list of resources, consulting, extra tips, cash back (in some cases), etc. to really incentivize them to take action now.

Last but not least with this topic of affiliate marketing, don't overthink how to get started or what topic you should start on! If you're spending more than a half hour thinking on this, you're likely overthinking it and hurting your chances of taking action that will result in a chance of profits flowing in. It's better just to start with something, even not the most ideal offer, than to spend days, weeks, months, or even years thinking about what might be the perfect way to start...

5.   4. Earn Money Blogging or Creating Videos: Ads

What this online business looks like

Do you enjoy writing? Do you have thoughts on a specific topic (or even on a broad range of topics)? Do you consider blogging or creating videos to be something enjoyable?

Lots of people put plenty of time into writing a blog or creating videos and building an audience with no end in sight to their efforts — they pursue this blog or videos, instead, simply because it is something they enjoy doing. What most of these people fail to realize, however, is that a lot of money can be made blogging or creating videos by simply populating them with ads!

What you need to get started

All you really need, in order to make money from ads on a blog or video, is a popular blog or YouTube channel! Some of you may have a popular blog already, with a dedicated audience you have been building for years. You may even have been wondering how you could squeeze some money out of your readers, in order for your efforts to actually be worthwhile in a monetary sense, without realizing that you never actually need to get your readers to pay for anything! Instead, you simply need to team up with any ad provider that will populate your site with targeted ads. In the case of videos, you can do the same by mentioning products (even affiliate links) within the video or having ads on the video on YouTube (although this typically doesn't pay as much as directly promoting offers yourself).

This is the best aspect of today's online culture! You do not need to collect ads from specific companies that have a specific product to market to your specific audience; instead, ad providers are able to place ads on your site that are specifically targeted to each viewer, based on their search history! While one visitor may be seeing an ad for a boutique clothing store, another visitor may be seeing an ad for a new video game. All you have to do, then, is figure out a way to build a popular blog or video channel!

What type of content to create and how

Most people either create useless content without a lot of value, or they simply don't create anything at all! One trick that can work wonders for blogs and videos is to do some research in your niche of interest, see what types of questions people are asking or searching for, target those keywords in the titles of your blog posts and videos, and then simply answer the questions! As a bonus, you can use affiliate marketing to promote various products as well in your recommendations.

A tactic that can work well without being overloaded with work is to brainstorm one question each week that a prospect might have, and then spend an hour or so answering that question in a blog post or video (or both) that you can put up on your blog and on YouTube and such. Simply by having the question in the title, you'll have a good chance of ranking for it in a lot of cases. And the best part is that these kinds of videos can stay up indefinitely and start to send you a steady flow of traffic without you having to do any additional work! So after a year, you could potentially have over fifty different pieces of content all driving you a steady flow of traffic that would be hands free at that point!

<u>What your expectations should be</u>

This is not an approach for the faint of heart. While you could easily put a blog in place in one day (while you could, in fact, put a blog in place in a matter of minutes – blogger.com is a great resource to set one up for free in minutes), it often takes months or even years to build a truly dedicated audience — a large audience that makes your blog a destination of theirs each and every day. If you enjoy blogging — if there is a particular area of public interest in which you enjoy sharing your thoughts (that is to say: if you enjoy blogging, and it is something you have been doing, or would be doing, even without any monetization plan), adding advertisements to your site can be a great way to turn this hobby into a way to start making plenty of money! But if blogging seems like it would be a chore, and if you would be doing it solely for the online business aspect of it, there are probably other approaches that would be better for you.

When it comes down to it, you need to ask yourself whether blogging feels like "work" or not. If blogging (writing or videos) seems like something fun and enjoyable — something you would enjoy doing even without pay — this is an excellent route to take.

6.   5. Earn Money Blogging / Creating Videos: Lead Generation

What this online business looks like

Another way to turn blogging or creating videos into a means to profit is to use a blog or videos as a tool for lead generation.

What is lead generation? Basically, it is exactly what it sounds like: efforts directed toward generating leads (with leads being, of course, the contact information of individuals who have not necessarily made a purchase yet, but who can be targeted for a purchase or a set of purchases down the road).

Lead generation is one of the most powerful forms of online commerce, and running a blog that is geared toward lead generation is one of the best ways to get the most out of your lead generation efforts. Blogs can be a great way to get prospects to sign-up straight to your list from the blog, whereas with videos on YouTube, for instance, you can encourage viewers to subscribe straight to your video channel there (for the purposes of promoting future offers, getting prospects to your own list outside of YouTube is much preferred, though).

For example: let's say you are writing a blog about successful online businesses. On this website you provide plenty of valuable information about succeeding online, and you also feature plenty of guest posts that focus on the same topic (with these guest posts serving a dual purpose: firstly, you get plenty of free content, and secondly, you get extra traffic to your site as these guest posters share the link with their audience; they benefit by being featured on your site and reaching your audience as a result, and you benefit by adding to the audience on your site and by not having to write all the content yourself). You are not using this blog to sell anything, but are instead using this blog simply to provide lots of valuable information. In fact, you are even giving away additional, premium content to those who visit your site ... they enter their email address, and this premium content that usually costs money is sent directly to their inbox for free — no gimmicks, no commitments.

Do you see what you just did? You now have an email address for every individual who requested that free, premium content. And not only do you have an email address ... but you also know that this email address belongs to someone who has an interest in this specific area!

As your free, information-based website continues to grow in popularity, your database of emails will grow as well, and you will be able to then use this list to intermittently send out special offers to (ready for this tie-in?) information products focused in the area they expressed an interest in before!

Of course, these can be information products you created yourself, or it can be information products for which you are an affiliate. Or it can even be for physical products, services, etc.. Either way, you will have a large email list of people who you know for certain are interested in this specific niche, and you will be able to use this email list to target these individuals with related products!

Building a subscriber list on YouTube is a little different. Instead of just having prospects sign-up directly for a free offer of yours and you having total control over the leads, YouTube allows you to have your viewers "subscribe" to your channel where they're more likely to automatically see your future videos and such when they visit YouTube. This obviously has its benefits, but you definitely want to be building your own list as well.

What you need to get started

All you really need to get started is a website (for a blog) and a topic on which you want to focus! By signing up for an account with GetResponse (the top email list management service), you will be able to start capturing email addresses — and as you start creating content yourself and gathering guest posts from others, you will be able to start seeing your email list grow before your eyes. Ideally I would recommend creating both blog posts and videos (for YouTube) at the same time, as it's like getting two birds with one stone and doubling your chances of exposure (if not more). And almost anyone can create a YouTube channel, throw up some videos, and get started fairly easily there (it doesn't have to be professionally shot).

What your expectations should be

This is a long-term game, as it's rare to build a massive list overnight this way (possible, but more rare). With that said, however, leads are the most powerful tool in any online entrepreneur's arsenal. No matter what you are doing online, lead generation should be one of your focuses, as there is no easier way to make money than to send a simple email to a loaded, targeted list that you have built over time! And once you have useful content out there that draws the prospects into joining your list, it's like a well oiled machine grabbing leads for free for you. Every piece of content or video is like part of a spider web hauling in prospects for you on autopilot to later market to. And even though it can be a slower start, once it gets going, it can be a huge benefit and a money making machine that you can tap into at will!

PART 2:

THE ONES YOU PROBABLY HAVEN'T THOUGHT OF

Now that we have looked at some of the businesses that would come to mind first for most successful online entrepreneurs, it is time to turn our attention to some of the "back burner" items, or the business ideas that most don't tend to think of yet can be incredibly lucrative and still easy to start!

Yes, these are online businesses that might not jump out to your basic online entrepreneur as the first thing they think about when it comes to online wealth creation, but these approaches are no less powerful. In fact, some of these businesses can create an even higher ceiling for success than the businesses listed in Part 1!

When it comes down to it, you must remember this when selecting an online business idea on which to turn your focus: the best business will always be whatever is the best business *for you*!

As we said in the introduction to Part 1: the main key to succeeding in online business (as is the case with any business) will be that you are willing to put in the effort required to make that business work. As long as you are willing to take the time to learn the ins and outs of how a business works, and are willing to then put in the effort required to be successful, there is no reason why you cannot turn *any* online business into a profitable one for you.

As you read through these next business ideas, determine whether or not any of them strike a chord with you. If one of these sounds like a business idea that will be perfect for you, go ahead and start taking strides toward making one of these businesses your own, and toward enabling this business to become your form of online wealth creation!

7.   6. Manage Social Media Profiles

What this online business looks like

One of the most important aspects for businesses these days is having a strong social media presence, as social media is where a great number of people spend a huge chunk of their time (are you guilty of that?). By having a strong social media presence, businesses are able to connect with customers and potential customers in a consistent, personable manner ... and by failing to have a strong social media presence, a business can quickly fall behind their competition. This is something most businesses understand these days — but what many businesses do not understand is what they should be doing in order to strengthen and enhance their social media presence. Because these businesses do not know how to handle social media on their own, they either botch their efforts, or they ignore social media entirely.

What's the other options for these businesses? They can hire out their social media management to a person or company that knows how to handle social media successfully.

What does this mean for you? Frankly, it means that if social media is something you enjoy and are good at, you can quickly and easily build a client base of your own — managing the social media elements of various small and mid-size businesses! Best of all, because so much of social media can actually be automated, this is not as large of a time commitment as most businesses seem to imagine it would be. In fact, there's social media managers out there that can charge hundreds of dollars a month for sometimes an hour or less of work a month … or thousands of dollars a month for only several hours of work. One of the resources mentioned at the start of this book can even help automate much of this for you!

The ability to charge premium prices here means that you only need just a small handful of clients to start making some serious money. Even one or two clients can be a good chunk of money, but just a few more can often replace the money most other full-time jobs normally make (but at a fraction of the time spent). And it's a service that the vast majority of businesses really need, and one that doesn't have to be hard to sell.

What you need to get started

All you really need, in order to get started in this area of business, is a bit of knowledge on social media and a strong sales pitch! In a single day, you could throw together a website on which you can promote yourself, and you can then start scouring the internet in search of small and mid-size businesses that seem to be lacking in their social media approach. Start approaching these businesses with a brief outline of what they should be doing differently on social media and of how you could help them execute this plan. You could even offer them a free consultation or a free week of social media service (or a free month if you want an unbeatable offer)! Once you turn this interest into a conversion, you will have a client who will pay you monthly to handle their social media —

and you will subsequently be able to schedule most of this social media activity in advance and enjoy all the free time you are left with after that!

What your expectations should be

Depending on how hard you are willing to hustle in picking up new clients, you could actually find that you have a strong client list within a few short weeks! Furthermore, if you do not feel like managing social media as your sole online enterprise, you could pick up just a couple clients, and could dedicate a small amount of time to the social media efforts of these clients each month while still having plenty of time free for other business ventures!

8.   7. Internet Research Firm

What this online business looks like

How often do you find yourself losing two hours as you simply wander around the Internet, looking up different things and reading different articles? One of the greatest benefits of the Internet is the vast amount of information and knowledge it makes available to anyone with the time to access and peruse it—but while this may be something you do simply to kill a couple hours, there are businesses that see Internet research as a tedious (and even overwhelming) task. These businesses will often outsource their research tasks to internet research firms.

What does it take to create an Internet research firm yourself? Honestly, you need nothing more than a website that describes your "firm" and details what it offers! With one such site set up, you will be able to start spreading the word about the site, and will be able to start picking up payment for doing what you typically do in your free time anyway: perusing the Internet for random information and knowledge!

What you need to get started

Obviously, you will need to get the word out there to various businesses that you are available for internet research jobs, so after you set up a website that establishes your place online, put together a list of businesses that may need research done, then approach each business with an email, letting them know that about your firm. Before long, you will start receiving work assignments from the businesses you have contacted — and it probably will not be long before you are receiving so many assignments that you are having to turn down more than you are able to actually accept!

You can also post ads up on job sites, classified ad sites (like Craigslist), etc. with your services offered. You can also easily expand this service by getting others working for you and you being a sort of middleman in all of this.

What your expectations should be

As with the social media management work, there is really no reason why you should be unable to build a strong client list in a short amount of time, as long as you are willing to put in the work to reach out to businesses and get the word out there about the services you offer!

Is internet research something you enjoy doing in your free time anyway? If so, you may as well start making money off this by doing this research for businesses that are in need of it! It's definitely more along the lines of trading time for money when you start out, but it's easy to start and there's extra opportunity for growing and profiting a lot more (without all the extra time put into it) if you grow it by taking on others to do the work for you like a firm or a middleman would.

9.   8. Freelance Writing

What this online business looks like

Content is the most important side of the internet. Without content, a website will not succeed, and while this is something most businesses realize, a massive majority of businesses are lost when it comes to content creation.

Because people tend to hear so often that there is "no money in writing," you may have failed to realize that the rise of the internet has caused a paradigm shift to occur. These days, there is lots of money in writing … simply because there is lots of money online, and one of the main ways to succeed online is with lots of content!

Another thing to realize is that you do not need to be a professional writer in order to make money with freelance writing. As long as you are a strong, competent writer, you will be able to make money in this area — and, of course, the more writing jobs you take on, the more practice you will gain in this area, and the stronger your work will be (which, of course, will lead to more jobs, and more money per job, as a result!). Even if you suck at writing, there's always ways where you can outsource the writing to writers and act as a middleman (more on that in the next tips section).

Extra Tips to Charge Way More and Work Less

The major downside with freelance writing is that you normally are trading time for money, but that doesn't have to be the case! There are two ways to get around this. The first one is that you can hire existing writers to do the work for you where you simply act as a middleman. Sites like Fiverr.com can have lots of writers willing to work for cheap (as well as Craigslist, freelance sites, etc.). Another way, which you can do the work both yourself or using an outsourcer instead, is to increase the perceived value and price points of your writing services (this can actually work well for any service). Instead of selling a writing service for articles, you can sell "articles / blog posts optimized for Google," which basically means that you target keywords in your title. This takes literally no extra time (or no extra cost) but can significantly increase the perceived value and price point that you can sell the service for.

You can step that up a notch by selling a "done for you" system where you put their whole blog and social media content on autopilot, or even step it up another notch by creating an entire blog with content from scratch that is optimized for the search engines and completely hands free for the buyer! You can outsource the blog creation, graphics, etc. for as little as $5 to $25, and then get five or so custom articles for $5 or so a piece, so for an all in cost of $50 or less (even if you get all that for $100 or less, this still works well), you have something that you can literally sell for $1,000 or more and seem like you have a steal of a deal! After all, what sounds better? Getting an article for $10 or getting a complete, hands free site pre-filled with content and optimized for the search engines for $1,000? A lot of business owners would pick the $1,000 option! And the best part is that the raw cost and work isn't proportionally more, but it turns your simple "article service" into something worth far more to them. And you can even up that even more by charging a monthly fee to continue to popular the blog and social media with content, so just a few sales can lead to a lot of money!

What you need to get started

The great thing about freelance writing is that you do not necessarily even need a website in order to get started! There are plenty of websites that connect people in need of freelance work with writers who provide such work. In fact, believe it or not, the best place of all to pick up freelance projects may very well be right on Craigslist, Facebook, Fiverr, etc. — which require no membership at all!

The critical component to picking up freelance writing work is a strong resume or ad that stands out from the pack. Don't have lots of writing experience just yet? No problem! Put together a strong writing resume that skirts around the fact that you do not have extensive experience in actual freelance writing — focusing instead on your skills and "what you provide to your clients." Often times all a prospect needs to see is one very well written relevant article that they like to want more of them (the resumes don't matter a ton).

As you continue to add jobs to your work history, you can add to your writing resume, mentioning the types of jobs you have taken on in the past, and the type of work you are comfortable doing. The longer you work in freelance writing, the more contacts you will build, and the easier it will be for you to pick up new freelance jobs with very little additional work on your part!

What your expectations should be

The sky is the limit when it comes to freelance writing, as more experience in this area will enable you to work more quickly, and will enable you produce a higher level of quality work. Working more quickly will mean that you are able to finish projects more quickly (thereby giving you more free time, or more time for additional projects), and as your quality increases, you will be able to increase what you charge for your work as well. And with the ability to outsource this work to other writers, add more value by creating more "done for you" offers, etc., the possibilities are truly endless. Ultimately, all of this leads to a place where freelance writing is a lucrative form of online business and wealth creation!

10. 9. WordPress Consulting And Design

What this online business looks like

"I don't know how to build a website."

This is what most people think when they are first getting started with their quest to find success through online business. What these people fail to realize, however, is that building a website on WordPress is one of the easiest things you will ever do! And while a basic WordPress website will not look like a professional website, it does not take long to figure out how to move from a basic WordPress site to a customized WordPress site that looks like a true, top-notch website.

Of course, for just about any form of making money online, you are going to ultimately want/need a good-looking website — a website that stands out from the pack and that looks professional and impressive — and as you learn how to work with WordPress, you will be able to build one such site for yourself. But what about taking this to the next step?

A lot of small businesses either have no website at all or have a website that is unattractive and unappealing. Furthermore, a lot of small businesses have websites that were built by a company that charges them for every change that needs to be made on the site — with these sites built on some sort of proprietary platform that allows for almost no customization at all. Any business that falls into any of these categories could use a well-designed WordPress website — and most of these businesses have no idea just how easy building one such website can be!

By taking a small amount of time to learn how to work with WordPress yourself, you will be able to then market your services to businesses in this area — either as a consultant for their WordPress site, or as a "web designer." Better yet, by building on a WordPress platform, you can train the business in how to run the website on their own, which will make you even more valuable to them, and will enable you to charge even more for an upfront setup fee, as these businesses will no longer have to pay a recurring website maintenance fee each month!

Extra Tips to Keep in Mind

This type of service doesn't just have to be for WordPress (even though that's the example given). You could, for instance, do a lot of the same thing with a free blog platform like Blogger.com, which is even easier for a novice to setup to start with (but slightly more limiting later). However, you could also apply this to virtually any platform out there! Whether it be blogging, shopify or other e-commerce platforms, e-mail marketing with autoresponders, etc.. There are tons of platforms that businesses just don't have the time or desire to learn, and you can use that to your advantage by specializing in them! The crazy part is that for a lot of these types of services, one can go from knowing nothing to being fairly well educated in them in under a day's time. Business owners often times just don't want to learn one more thing, even if it doesn't have to be difficult, which is why that works to your advantage. It's also important to note that you also don't have to be the one doing the work, as just like with any other service, you can outsource even that as well!

What you need to get started

All you need is a good-looking WordPress site of your own! Once you have this, you can start building a list of businesses that could benefit from your services, and you can then start approaching these businesses and "selling yourself" to them! It could not be any easier to start getting "web design" or "website consulting" work, especially if you decide to outsource most / all of the work as you start your own little "firm" so to speak!

What your expectations should be

Because web design and website maintenance can seem like some sort of voodoo or impenetrable magic to many small business owners, you will find that "web design and website maintenance" can be a very lucrative business — even if you are simply building websites on a WordPress platform! As with any form of business, it may take a little while for you to build your client base to the level you want, but once you are able to start growing your list of clients, you will be able to make a great deal of money in this area! And once your clients have their sites, there's lots of other services that you could look into selling them as well to exponentially grow your business even larger much faster!

11.   10. Become A Business Service Provider

What this online business looks like

There are so many services small and mid-size businesses need:

- Web design

- Search engine optimization

- Adwords maintenance

- Facebook ad management

- Newsletter management

- Social media management

- Content creation

- List management

- PR Service

These are just a few of the services that are vital to the success of most such businesses, but that these businesses nevertheless fail to handle in a proper and effective manner.

While some of our other sections focused on handling some of this work yourself (which is certainly a path worth pursuing if some of these are things you enjoy doing), you should also realize that you can sell such services without ever actually doing any of the work yourself!

Because there are so many people who are chasing the idea of being able to make money online, from the comfort of their own home, there is really no shortage of available freelancers in just about any area you can think of. What does this mean for you? Basically, it boils down to this: if you are able to sell these services to businesses, you can then outsource the actual work to freelancers. All you do, then, is act as the middleman — taking on the projects from businesses, but assigning the projects to freelancers!

As you do this for a little while, you will begin to build a stable of freelancers that you work well with — freelancers who provide quality work in a timely manner — and your reputation will grow with businesses as well, as an "online business service provider that does quality work in a timely manner," all while never actually doing any of the work yourself! You get paid for the projects; a portion of the payment goes to the people who do the work; you get to keep the rest for yourself as profit!

Another huge advantage you have here is that several of these services can be managed almost hands free by using some of the tools and resources mentioned at the start of this book, so you can do an "expert service" that normally would cost thousands of dollars and involve a ton of work without having to do much work yourself! To make things even better, most of these topics can be learned in a day or less to start out (longer to master, but you don't have to be a master to help 99% of businesses out there), or they can be easily outsourced to freelancers who just deal with that one topic every single day!

There are ad management experts out there who charge over $7,000 / month per client! And there are social media experts who charge $2,000 / month or more out there per client. There's also list managers out there who take a cut (as high as 50%) of all the sales generated from a list simply for managing and mailing offers to the list. There's PR managers (basically getting free exposure on news sites, blogs, in the media, etc. for your clients) that can literally get paid thousands of dollars just by submitting news stories, blog posts, or articles out there. And don't think that you can't do any of these things! Someone can literally take an article or blog post written by them or a client, submit it to several news sites, blogs that accept guest blog posts, etc. on behalf of their client and have a "PR service." A client of ours once said that he sold a client of his on a million dollar package for his PR service, even though he said it was very similar to what he does for clients that he charges in the $500 to $5,000 range for (just on a bit of a larger scale).

There truly is nothing special about any of these kinds of services that would limit you from jumping into them. And when a single client can literally make more than a lot of full-time jobs make, the bar doesn't have to be set real high to have financial freedom there if you go about it well. It's worth taking a day or so to explore any of these that are of most interest to you.

Extra Tips

Keep in mind that similar to the example giving in the freelance writing section, you can increase the perceived value of any of these services that you sell. Instead of an article writing service, you could be selling a PR service where you submit the article on behalf of your client to other blogs and news sites that accept guest posts. That can up your perceived value from $10 to $1,000 easily, yet the actual work isn't really that much more.

The best part is that you also don't have to be the one doing the work, as you can take any of these "basic" types of services offers from others on freelance sites, Craigslist, Fiverr, etc. and turn them into your own premium level service (or combine them) and sell them for top dollar without being the one having to do all the fulfillment! You can even list these premium services on other ad sites, find prospects out there asking relevant questions on your service top that you can answer and point them in your direction, or even reach out directly to or advertise to the best prospects out there, especially since your margins will be so much higher than the vast majority of your competition.

Another huge tip that can explode your profits here is to create a premium level service that you then approach other related, but not competing, companies with and offer to white label your service(s) for them! White labeling is where you allow them to sell your services as though they are their own, as well as allow them to either charge a lot more or take a big cut of your sales as their own. The more hands free you make it for other companies to sell your own services as their own, the more likely they are to take you up on it and sell them as their own. You're just the one in the background making a lot of money without having to do any of the marketing! A single white label deal here literally could be a business all by itself, and it can make many, many times more than what you could possibly make by marketing on your own.

What you need to get started

As with other forms of freelance work or business management work — forms we talked about in the previous sections, in which you would be doing the work yourself — you need a good website and a good sales pitch, one that will get businesses to feel tempted to jump on board with you, and then you need a list of businesses that might benefit from your service (which you can compile yourself through some simple Internet research). You do not even need to enlist any freelancers until you have actually been hired for a job! "Can you do such-and-such?" This is what businesses will ask you, and your answer will always be "Yes." Because, after all, you will always be able to find someone who will be able to do whatever task you have been hired for within reason!

A great way to start out, especially if you're more new to this, is to have an "unbeatable offer / hook" to get prospects interested. This can be a free trial of your services, a big free bonus if they join (like making a free Facebook page for Facebook ad management … or a free blog with a monthly content service). It can involve taking some extra time or money at the start, but it's just a numbers game, as if even a couple turn into big clients for you, it can all be worthwhile!

What your expectations should be

The more work you pick up in this area — and the more you continue to return good work to those who have hired your company — the more work you will find is coming your way with no additional effort. This ultimately becomes the perfect business model, where all you have to do is say "Yes" to whatever project comes your way, and then find someone who can do the work, all without ever having to lift a finger on the work itself at any point in time!

12.   11. Affiliate Marketing: Reviews

What this online business looks like

Some of the first business ideas mentioned in this book involved affiliate marketing. This is just a unique twist on that, which literally anyone can do with only a limited amount of time each week!

Basically, as you've already learned, affiliate marketing is where you get paid a commission for someone buying something through your affiliate link. But there are several different ways that you can profit off of this. You can read up on the prior sections to go over the basics of affiliate marketing if you skipped past them.

With this twist on affiliate marketing, you'd basically write product reviews for products that you're already an affiliate for (or could easily be an affiliate for). If you already have used various products or know a lot about them, this would obviously be super easy for you to do! But there are tricks to doing this even if you've never used the product before or even if you don't know anything about it (more on that shortly in the tips section here…).

What you need to get started

All you really need to get started is to ideally search for products that you already know a bit about, that have high demand, and that have a decent affiliate program that pays a good chunk to you. Sites like

Amazon.com, Clickbank.com, etc. can be good places to start, but you can also just search for "[product name] affiliates" (or similar terms) and find lots of private affiliate programs in a quick Google search.

After signing up to be an affiliate, you then need to create the review! This can either be done on a blog or site (like blogger.com for free – super easy to use and setup a blog there) or via a video that you can post on YouTube. Then in either case, the format is usually similar. You start by having a product review type keyword in your title (like "[product name] review," or "[product 1] vs. [product 2] review" – there are literally dozens to hundreds of similar ones) – the less results on Google and YouTube on page one with the exact keyword in their title tag (the blue link in the results), the better. Then you have a short summary of the product with a couple sentences, followed by a pros and cons list, followed by a short conclusion, and finally followed by a call to action containing your affiliate link where they can get a good deal on it.

Reviews shouldn't be terribly long! Nor should they only focus on just positives (those look fake), but they do need to give a clear and decisive answer as to what you think the reader / listener should do (aka buy the product or buy which one based on what?)!

Then it's just a matter of getting reviews out there and either waiting for them to get ranked for traffic to come to you, or you finding leads out there on forums, Q&A sites, blogs, etc. where you can post relevant information with a link to your in-depth review to help jumpstart your traffic..

Tricks to making this easier

It helps a ton to have affiliate offers that not only are popular, but that also have good commissions. High priced offers often times can make you a lot more money because the commissions typically are much higher, and it's often times just as easy (if not easier) to rank for these terms over smaller priced items that are also popular.

Another fear that a lot of people have is that they think they have to own all the products that they want to write reviews for. Although this can help, it isn't necessarily the case! A trick that works really well here is for you to write a "review of reviews out there" and spend a half hour or so reading all the other reviews out there, and then summarize all those reviews with the pros and cons and your own conclusion about what the reader / viewer should do (buy or not or buy in which cases). You can even say in the review you write itself that you're reviewing and summarizing all the other reviews out there, which makes it way easier on them. People love saving time, and this can not only save them time, but it can make you seem like the most logical review to base their decisions on!

What your expectations should be

Although it's possible that a single review can make a lot of money fast, typically it takes time and lots of reviews for things to really start ramping up. That's why you'll want to set a little time aside each week to either write a new review or spend a little time seeking out prospects asking relevant questions that you can drive them to your review to gain more traffic and links.

Spending even just an hour or so a week (even if you skip some) can help you to start building up a massive amount of reviews. And you can choose to do these reviews on a written blog or just verbally on a video (or both – even better) – whichever you're most comfortable with. This can be a great way to earn some extra income without having to commit a ton of time or thought into, so it's one of the easiest ways to dive into making money online when you're just starting out.

13.   12. Affiliate Marketing: Free Services

What this online business looks like

We've already gone over a few different ways to make affiliate marketing work in different business models! This next one is a very cool twist that lets you provide an unbeatable offer for free while still making a lot of money!

Essentially this is where you pick affiliate offers that are popular and pay higher commissions than normal, but then look for a service that you can offer for free where you either recommend the affiliate product or almost force them to buy it to take advantage of your free service. For instance, I had a service where I'd help people find good deals on diamonds. Instead of selling diamonds myself or charging for my services, which would be unlikely to get buyers with all the information and competitors out there, I simply offered a free service where I'd help see if either the diamonds they were looking at were good deals, or if I could find some better deals for similar or better diamonds out there for less. I would then search popular diamond sites that I was an affiliate for, find some legitimately awesome deals that matched what they were looking for, and then recommended the exact diamonds with my affiliate link. Occasionally I would also be able to promote a coupon offer via my affiliate link to save them even more. This allowed me to offer a service for free, which was an attractive offer to others, yet it'd allow me to get paid often times hundreds of dollars per sale on the backend (sometimes even more).

Another example here would be if you were in the forex trading niche (or any kind of investing niche). Instead of selling a course on how to trade in the forex market … you could simply offer your advice for free, say you'll walk them through their first investment personally, and all they have to do is sign-up for a free forex trading account (which in some cases would pay hundreds of dollars per sign-up) so that you're advising them on how to do any trading through that. It's a win-win for all involved!

What you need to get started

All you really need to get started is to think of higher end affiliate offers that are popular, and then do some research to see what kinds of questions, issues, etc. people have related to that. Then look to create a free service to help solve their problems. Then you simply need to advertise or mention your "free" service where your potential prospects are hanging out (forums, blogs, Q&A sites, etc.). If your service is genuine and useful, you'll get takers!

You can step it up a notch by creating a website, blog, or video talking about your free service, the benefits of using your free service, etc.. In almost no time, you'll have an unbeatable offer that your competition literally likely can't compete with because very few will want to offer a free service back when so many think the only way to profit is to charge money for these things.

Tricks to ramp this up

Besides just using this free service to directly sell your recommended affiliate offers, you can do another twist on this in a few different ways. First, you can give out a free service as a bonus if someone buys a particular affiliate offer of yours. For instance, if you're an affiliate for a high end course on how to get better at tennis (assuming you know a lot about that niche), you could offer a free service where you'll analyze a video of them playing to give them a few pointers. Or if you're an affiliate for a high-end course on Facebook ads, you could offer a free service where you create their first ad or manage their ad for free for a certain amount of time, which can work out great for you, as not only can you incentivize your prospects to buy through your affiliate link, but your bonus free service can even be a trial that leads into a recurring paid service that perhaps makes you even more money in the long run! This trick is often way overlooked by highly effective.

What your expectations should be

Affiliate marketing can be great by itself even in its most basic form, but by sprucing up your affiliate recommendations with free services or bonuses, you can really skyrocket your affiliate earnings. However, you absolutely must make sure that your free service provides value and is something that people want. If you can do that, you can get prospects lining up to take advantage of your free service that others charge for (and still making you a lot of money).

It all comes down to making sure that you have an offer that stands out from your competition. And what better way to do that than by offering something for free that others normally charge for?

14.   In Conclusion

What we hope you get out of this

You've read a dozen different types of businesses that you can easily start within a day, with many of them ones that can have dozens of variations or different kinds of businesses within each of them. The key is to pick one or two that stand out to you the most to start with, and then take some kind of action!

It doesn't matter if it's perfect or if you utterly fail at your first attempt! The difference between being a success vs. being a failure is that the successful people take action, fail quickly, make adjustments, and then jump right back into things.

Regardless if you're brand new and never ran a business yourself, or if you're an experienced entrepreneur already making millions, we hope that these different business ideas can at least get your creative juices flowing to help you either grow or expand your business in multiple different ways. Once you become successful with any of these models, you can either then replicate them over and over, or take on some of the other business ideas here to continue growing your online businesses.

To help with your journey, at the start of this book and on the next page, we offer you a few different resources and tools for you to check out to help, including ways to help automate some of these businesses more! Enjoy!

15. To Learn More

Remember to claim your Free Bonus!

Www.tolgacakir.com/bonus

16.   About the Author

Tolga CAKIR

Tolga Cakir is an author, Digital Marketing Consultant, entrepreneur, journalist, life coach and adventurer on a lifelong mission to empower people to achieve their dreams and step into their best versions. Deeply driven and dedicated, he presently serves as the CEO and Founder of Waanaa, Black Eagle Publishing & Media, and London Business Networking Group. As a writer, he has authored the Amazon best-selling book "How to Start an Online Business in 7 Steps."

Over the course of his multifaceted career, Tolga has gained extensive startup experience and has completed various training. Armed with that valuable firsthand knowledge, he strives to impart upon aspiring entrepreneurial minds the tools they need to create and sustain thriving businesses. In addition to his proven expertise and deep-rooted passion for helping others succeed, he received a BSc (Hons) in Business Information Systems. He is also a Certified Master Transformational Coach & Leader, Professional Speaker, Master Ericksonian Hypnotist, and Master Next Generation NLP practitioner. Tolga loves to travel and always seeks and works on inspiring new innovations and ideas.

http://www.tolgacakir.com/

www.ingramcontent.com/pod-product-compliance
Lightning Source LLC
Chambersburg PA
CBHW021608210326
41599CB00010B/656